Cellos in Hell

With best wishes to
Rosemary
(fellow writes).

Jim C. Wilson
March 2006.

Cellos in Hell

Jim C. Wilson

Chapman Publications
1993

Published by
Chapman
4 Broughton Place
Edinburgh EH1 3RX
Scotland

The publisher acknowledges the financial assistance of the
Scottish Arts Council in the publication of this volume.

A catalogue record for this volume is
available from the British Library.
ISBN 0-906772-45-1

Chapman New Writing Series
Editor Joy Hendry
ISSN 0953-5306

© Jim C. Wilson 1993
Jim C. Wilson is hereby identified as the author of
this work in accordance with Section 77 of the
Copyright, Design and Patents Act 1988.

All rights are strictly reserved.
Requests to reproduce the text in whole or in part
should be addressed to the publisher.

Some of these poems have previously appeared in
2Plus2, Acumen, Cencrastus, Chapman, Encounter, Iron, Lines Review, Northlight, Orbis, Outposts, Poetry & Audience, Poetry Canada Review, Poetry Show—Two, Poetry Street—One, Radical Scotland, She, Spectrum, The Honest Ulsterman, The Literary Review, The Rialto, The Scotsman, Understanding, West Coast Magazine, Weyfarers, and in
The Loutra Hotel *(Making Waves Press)*
others have been broadcast by BBC Radio Scotland or STV

Designed & typeset by Peter Cudmore
Cover design by Fred Crayk

Printed by
Mayfair Printers
Print House
William Street
Sunderland
Tyne and Wear

Contents

Introduction
Cellos in Hell

- Cellos 11
- Sarah And Teddy 12
- At The Public Baths 13
- Solitary Way 14
- A Small Affair 15
- The Student Flat 16
- At Abercorn 17
- The Last Lie 18
- Alastair 19
- Mother 20
- No Life At All 21
- Ambulances 22
- Beyond Horizons 23
- The Hunters 24
- Spring Visitors 25
- A Road To The Isles 26
- Last Summer In The Hebrides 27
- The Bridge 28
- Prayer For A Journey 29
- The Loutra Hotel 30
- Ulysses Resting At Corfu Airport 31
- At The Turkish Butcher's Shop 32
- The Edge Of The Lake 33
- Paris Notes 34
- Break 35

Contents *(continued)*

Oradour 36
At Wordsworth's Cottage 37
Irina 38
I Fear 39
The Catch 40
Travelling 41
Going To Write 42
The Fly In The Poetry Book 43
Creative Writing 44
Evening Out 45
He Once Was A German Lad 46
Golgotha 47
You Will Be Remembered 48
The Dove 49
Dried Flowers 50
Leaving The Supermarket 51
Wintertime 52
How Will I Know Spring? 53
Sun And Candlelight 54
Out In The Suburbs 55
The Public Gardens Were Busy 56
In The Garden 57
The Specialist 58
Gent 59
The Night Gates 60
The Beasts 61
Dream 62

Introduction

I find Jim C Wilson's poems subtle yet unpretentious, humorous yet realistic. Although written in English, not Scots, they frequently remind me of another Edinburgh poet, Robert Garioch.

Wilson's education was entirely in Edinburgh and most of his varied working life has also been centred in Edinburgh. He spent a year in insurance before going to university. During the vacations he was a school janitor and barman. After teacher-training he lectured for over nine years at Telford College of Further Education. He imparted, among other subjects, Liberal Studies to students from a variety of vocational courses as well as SCE candidates. At the age of thirty-three Wilson took the risk of becoming a full-time writer. This led to his doing part-time jobs such as labourer and market-researcher. He also worked as interviewer and researcher with Edinburgh Old Town Oral History Project before he began to win grants and residencies as a writer. These experiences help to give authenticity to the content of his poems and a depth of understanding to his imagination.

The Edinburgh solidity of Wilson's background is detectable in his approach to poetry. There is a quality I would describe as *unflinching* in his work, whether it be the stark choices with which life confronts us, the psychological intensities of childhood and adolescence ('Sarah and Teddy'), the bleakness of widowhood, illness, old age and death; paltriness and tawdriness in Scottish sexual *mores* ('A Small Affair') or the cruelty and depravity of the human race ('Oradour').

Despite this unflinching quality, however, there is also compassion and humour: "Don't bring me, please,/ your fish knives and forks," ('Mother'). This poem begins with an amused tolerance of the mother's wish to keep the unused silver fish knives and forks in the family but ends with the admission that "they cut and tear my heart." Again, witnessing or experiencing the slow loss of joy, the gradual freezing into death, the trivialisation of literature or the insanities created by tourism, Wilson is able to sympathise and bring out the ironies. 'The Public Gardens Were Busy' begins with gurgling babies and ends with crows and gaunt dogs, which "began to copulate." So life begins again and again despite adversities and in whatever manner.

Acceptance of harsh realities, preferring the "lonely moan" of cellos in hell to harps and "soft drifting clouds of dreams" ('Cellos') leads on to more profound poems such as 'How Will I Know Spring?' where the hardships of winter are understood as essential for hope of thaw and re-awakening: "I can't live/ without rebirth; I wait for winter's claw." This is no new sentiment for poetry but is *made new* in this modern poem that actually invokes "iron hardness" when January is "mild".

This toughness, this enjoyment almost of "iron hardness" is characteristically Scottish. It is equally characteristic that this is often a mask or shell for uncertainties and fears. But Wilson does not try to escape from facing up to this fact either. He knows his crablike qualities, his fear of drowning out of his depth, out of control, his dread of ambulances, his "panic at the thought of travelling far." The thought, for the imaginative person, is often worse than the experience and Wilson *does* travel, with an amused, detached eye absorbing and recording, whether it be in the Hebrides, Paris or Corfu airport.

Wilson is not afraid to use the first person in his poetry, knowing that poets who think they can escape from their own voice into a second or third person are ultimately deluding themselves. All are poetic devices. The self as agent, as creator must be an "I" even if completed, as Buber showed, in the I-Thou. As creator, the poet inevitably makes the world out of words in his or her own image.

Jim C. Wilson, from his solid Edinburgh base, creates a stony world where people nevertheless keep renewing themselves and travel bravely on the single track. "Prayer for a Journey" is a prayer for us all on life's way and for the dangerous, often lonely journey of the poet.

Tessa Ransford
August 1992

For Mik.

For the writers (on pages and in person)
who have helped me hear the cellos –
and the harps.

For Joy Hendry with thanks
for continuing encouragement.

Cellos

There must be cellos in hell:
that lonely moan could

not be made by angels. Harps
are for streams, starbright,

summery – or soft drifting
clouds of dreams. You can

dance rejoicing at the blasts
of seven golden

trumpets announcing Judgement
Day. I'll step to the

different echoes from a cracked
drum; I'll take the dull

fires and the lonely moan of
the cellos in hell.

Sarah And Teddy

In the empty house Sarah took
Teddy in her arms. She forced
Mummy's lipstick to his stubborn
cloth mouth then made him look
in the mirror; Teddy was shocked
but said nothing. Sarah slipped the black
plastic lid from the pale cold cream,
checked the bedroom door was locked
then pressed the white softness hard down
into Teddy's yielding fur. He
grew limp yet slidy and shiny
as lino. Face powder hid his frown.

"That bear was bloody dear!" yelled Mummy
and slapped her daughter round the head.
"No tea for you until you've cleaned it
and then you'll go straight off to bed!"

In the bathroom Sarah clutched
greasy Teddy in her arms.
Gently she lowered his bulk
into the water
and kept him under.
"You're out of harm's
way now. No need to sulk."
Then, as an afterthought, "I
christen thee Mummy," as bubbles
rose to caress
the soft down of her arms.

At The Public Baths

I paid 1/9 for a crucifix
and wore it to the Baths. The teddy-boys
echoed Presley's perfect songs, getting kicks,
as they stroked their high quiffs dry. Shower noise,
pipe rattle, steam gasps and me, at ten, white
as rice-pudding, proud in trunks of satiny
purple and gold, thrusting my way through bright
light warm green waves, my eager limbs skinny
like milk-straws. The silvery chain clung to my
throat as I mouthed an Elvis pout; a boy,
I stood in the Shallow End. I eyed the High-
diving Board, felt the purest soaring joy
of taking off. "Next week, perhaps," I thought.
My cold cross dripped; my trunks felt cold and taut.

Solitary Way

Some said the Army was his death.
But, head shorn, uniformed,
and every mother's perfect son,
he rose again, warming wooden hearts.

Blue suede shoes were left behind;
through his celluloid years
and years he danced on sand,
nibbled pills and crooned.

In a cold half-empty picture-house
I kept vigil as he sleepwalked
(with wholesome girls in big bikinis)
through crass resorts and America.

And now, lost in middle-age,
as gates shudder and close,
I understand his falling,
would have him rising yet again.

I'd have him return
if even just to sing soft rhymes
to trained children and grinning dogs
in Eden on Hawaii.

A Small Affair

The back of her coat went up and down, up
and down against the hard brick wall, the hard
brick wall, the damp hard brick wall of Tollcross
car park. " Please don't hurt," she sighed. He didn't.

Her eyes closed against the dark; her mouth fell
open, gulping air and spits of drizzle.
The car lights leapt up in arcs like rainbows
as he stared down at her rapt stranger's face.

Thuds from the disco arrived on the wind
as sweating, tiring, he came out of time.

"Thank you," he whispered, mechanically.
She smiled. "Will you phone?"
He promised he would. But
he didn't.

Later, she tried to count the cost as she
surveyed the marks on her new winter coat;
she told her friend how good it had been. And
how, after some cleaning, things would be fine.

The Student Flat

The electric fire's one bar glowed
dully, half-smothered, its dust skin
of talc holding back the heat. In
a far-distant corner the dark

morning was ruffled by the hoarse
scrape of your tinny tranny; you'd
painted its case with flowers. Should
I wake you? Condensation dropped

down the black window glass like cold
tears; the thin curtains couldn't meet,
didn't quite fit. You slept, the sheet
wound round your strange nakedness. Cars

and buses edged into the dawn.
I saw two sticky coffee mugs,
some underclothes slumped on worn rugs.
An inch of cider still remained,

half-accusing. The staleness of the
spreading ashtray clung to the dead
air and my skin. Your single bed
sank in the middle and I ached

for you in the pale fireglow in
that old house full of strangers. I
woke you for the new term. Your sigh
was a little girl's; you blinked and

were surprised to see me that dawn
in 1968 when rain
made the roofs shine and I had lain
beside you in a night as brief

as a smile. The room was filled for
me with wonder as I am now
when I blink with surprise at how
you were so prepared to allow

me to stay that first October
night and then these twenty years.

At Abercorn

The churchyard is held in the breath of the sea;
the grass is nipped by frost.

A red sun shines its beam through the trees;
so little daylight remains.

A crow goes clattering across the slates;
smoke from smouldering leaves is rising.

I see us fifteen years ago, together,
reading names on gravestones.

Like ghosts in spring, those two young folk;
blossom dropped in the morning breeze.

I close the gate; I blow on my fingers
and know that I am more the ghost.

The Last Lie

On days when the cancer was worse and Dad
sat limp as a damp flannel, he would need
his greying face shaved. "I'm not so bad
today," he claimed as I sat shrinking from the deed.
The razor scuffed across his cheek; no good.
He was difficult to approach; the angle was wrong.
Some more soft soap might do the trick. "Would
you stop?" he said. "That's fine, that's fine son."
He wasn't shaved at all but Mother rinsed
his face while I feigned a reason to leave.
"I'll be better tomorrow," he said. I convinced
myself he would be: we all wanted a reprieve.
Two years of pain finished in a hospital bed
with the last lie. "He went peacefully," a nurse said.

Alastair

In teddy-bear picnic times the grown-up
boy led everywhere;
if I went down to the woods by day
I'd not have to go there alone.

Like him I'd escape in great fretwork planes,
zoom in the giantest Meccano cars.
Nine years behind, I trailed in his chaos
of socks and grey flannels, bike bits and baffies.

And like him I learned to stand sardonic:
a cool, worldly-wise, oh-so-detached observer.
But I never knew that he went in disguise
and like me had panic behind his eyes.

The man stopped leading; he must have got lost.
I think he went down to the woods alone.
And then for hours he spouted blood;
a big, pale babe in a forest of wires.

He cried out for help but no one could lead;
the drink had dissolved my brother's insides.
And I only knew the grown-up boy,
could only touch a dead man's finger.

Mother

Don't bring me, please,
your fish knives and forks.
I've seen that they're lovely,
they haven't been used,
and I know they've been in the box
since your silver anniversary.

I know you feel old and unwell
and you want me to have them,
your fish knives and forks;
you don't want anyone else
to get them when you're gone.
I know.

But I feel mortal enough already
and they cut and tear my heart,
your fish knives and forks.

No Life At All

"Have no regrets when I'm gone," said Mum. "This
is no life at all." Slowly and slower
she got to the shops, cooked twelve years of meals
for one, and didn't believe in it all,

she said. We found her lying by the sink
where, over fifty years before, she'd scrubbed
my brother's nappies till she shone. We cleared
soft biscuits, and snaps of unknown babies.

Ambulances

They come, they come, the ambulances.
They hasten Christ to his hanging;
they hurry Judas to his tree.

The streets all scream with ambulances
that keep coming for my father
who has loose pyjamas and hair like dust.

I hear the dark owl-hoot
of a distant steam train, out of sight:
my brother's ambulance is arriving early.

And louder than sadness, faster than winter,
our own are coming down every street.
They are white as a dawn of snowdrops.

And which of us will watch for the coming?
Who will be listening behind the screens?
Who will have the anxious, wrinkling heart?

I fear the crying of ambulances
for one of us must one day sit
with tears dropping like dead petals.

They come, they come, the ambulances.

Beyond Horizons

 The swimmer's lungs shout loud as thunder;
sea-fingers slide into his throat;
the salt bites sharp as shark-teeth.
He has been helmsman; he has been pilot;
as skipper he thrust his craft between starfish
and planets; he never followed sunset down.
 Now he recalls the sailor-boy
forever on beaches bigger than skies;
the soft young crabs reeled over his skin,
as mother and father, his horizons,
basked above the shoreline, like leviathans.
 He recalls his mate the golden one;
they buoyed each other up
when midnight storms unfurled the sails,
made them crack like splintering bones.
 But now he can't hold back the tide;
it's him alone, and all at sea.
Yet he'd take the ocean into his palms
and play with it like grains of salt.
 A child's spade slices through the sand
as rainbows rush on ever upward.

The Hunters

This forest's dark; thorns rip at our hearts;
and no-one's left to lead us out.
But even black moons have their radiance –
and unicorns *will* nuzzle your palms.

We're tired; mouths taste of vinegar.
Sadness and ash lie on our eyes.
But smell the greenness of November;
let's swoop on streaks of life, like owls.

Spring Visitors

The seals slid onto an edge
of Scotland. Grey and sleek
they were, on shining sandbanks,
taking a rest from the deeps.

We watched, we stared in the sun,
in the wind, eyes watering as we
strained for some insight,
a glimpse into the lives of seals.

Bodies arced through clouds of foam;
dark heads hovered on the tide.
A good spot perhaps for a fill
of fish, mating or just wallowing.

Were they, like the trippers, enjoying
the warmth, a change? Would rituals
be altered in the endless screams
of Leuchars' gleaming fighter-planes?

A Road To The Isles

A thread of ants,
coloured corpuscles in a long thin vein,
we're bypassing Loch Rannoch,
tailbacking through Glencoe.

High hawks are windscreen specks;
we motor fast over shortbread scenes.
Cascades hang in Kodak splendour;
the tar is trimmed with heather tangle.

Our Fiats, Volvos, Datsuns, Fords
flow swiftly by Glenfinnan.
We're a winding wire in a wilderness,
with so very, very far to go.

Last Summer In The Hebrides

July; the sodden peat bogs suck me down
as stumbling, squelching, I cross this dark isle
of brown, of green. Fast Atlantic clouds frown
and loom ahead of me in threats, in guile.
Behind me loll the rusting caravans,
roped to the earth, tied down with ancient stones;
spearwort and orchid force their wild advance
to weave and bloom through an old bus's bones.
The grocer's van did not arrive today
and letters came late from the world. It might
be the strange warm wind that made Angus say
there'd be no fishing, as he watched for light.

On the beach terns scream and I turn to stare
at cattle standing rigid in the glare.

The Bridge

Grey grasses, mists, hills; late afternoon skies
and the drowned valley, a dark reservoir.

The stone tower breaks the endless surface;
screams of gulls slice at the powerhouse hum.

The bridge to the tower is straight, is long;
cold waters pull beneath its rattling slats.

Winds and drizzle curve against us; we step
onto the bridge, finger its wet metal.

The bridge is the blue of warm promenades,
blue of loud fairgrounds, but hung in lead grey.

We travel the bridge in slow single file;
gulls get wilder; the tower grows; it grows.

But you stop. "It's a bad dream," you call out.
The mist is settling on your face, your hair.

I walk the shining bridge into the grey.
Does it sway? Am I safe? The gulls all watch.

At last I touch the tower door. Locked. Hard.
I must get back across that emptiness.

I look for you along the bridge. You've gone.
What temporary refuge have you found?

Prayer For A Journey

Wrong lane; turning. Stopping; clammer; clog.
The streets, the roads, the avenues clot;
the circulation froths and dribbles.
I follow the backs of hostile necks,
am followed by glinting spectacles.

Let me flow on a single-track road,
turn left for the ocean or right for the sky.
At passing-places strangers wave and smile,
then it's round the mountain, into the sun.
Let heather part as night comes pure and black.

Right now I would rest at a passing-place
but the single-track road gets harder to find.

The Loutra Hotel

On Nisyros there stands an old hotel;
once white, it now rests, peeling, by its black
seaside of boulders. A warm sulphur smell
embalms the place, entering every crack.
Above, hot dead slopes of volcanic ash
support a knotted maze of silvery
pipes (which rise like bulging veins). A deep gash
spits out the waters from an artery
beneath the rocks. On slabs of cold grey stone
the afflicted and old are sluiced, wiped, turned
and pray they'll be cured. In gowns white as bone,
nuns move through Loutra hotel. I smelled burned
fish from the dining-room. A few guests ate;
others, silently, seemed content to wait.

Ulysses Resting At Corfu Airport

His gold chain snakes through the greying scrub
that sprawls on his torso of glistering bronze.
He gleams away (amongst the fag-ends)
almost nude, as though he would show scars.
And, oh, there will be stories to tell.
All challenges have been met and vanquished
face to face: foreign waiters conquered,
the Scottish girl he screwed. Now even
his stormy bowels are deadly still.
He sucks in smoke from a duty-free, exploring,
gaze narrowing, the hazy tarmac horizon.
He'll return next year to the Paradise Villa;
but now his sun-cream tube is empty; he
squeezes out wet air. Stroking his dark forearm,
he turns towards the sinking sun
and dreams of his Penny in Wigan.

At The Turkish Butcher's Shop

We exchanged scraps of language: thank you,
beefsteak, three hundred grams. We thought
we'd got to know a local.
Better than the brochures!

And when we asked for mince, he grinned,
flipping steak into his steel machine;
cleanly, electrically, it shredded the meat,
shredded his finger, the flesh, the bone.

Waiting for an ambulance, he held up
the stump, as though he would point
at the sky; he held it like a glass of tea
he wouldn't spill for the life of him.

We thought he might die (and just for our mince)
as, starting to faint,
his loose old trousers slipping off,
he was helped into the ambulance.

We made enquiries; we were concerned.
Yet no one seemed too bothered:
"That happens to butchers,"
a Turkish woman told us.

And after three days,
sporting a bloodied grey bandage,
he was slicing meat again,
saying thank you.

For what was a finger when
he still had his job?
We hadn't known the Turk at all,
how he couldn't afford, like us, to care.

We went each day and bought our meat,
though speaking as if from a distance,
in scraps,
like the strangers we were.

The Edge Of The Lake

Dust on dust; heat thickened around us. We
bumped together, aliens in an ancient
landscape. Our Turkish taxi growled between
dry fields; a trapped fly whined behind our necks.

In the end we reached that place of colours
firm as stone: nothing muted and nothing
northern. The freshwater lake was brimming
with sky. We gorged on pure white flesh of carp.

We were there for the tombs; they lay rippling,
gurgling, beneath the surface. Time then tide
had scoured them out: gaping carved-rock coffins,
welcoming as warm baths, our journey's end.

I froze all in a photograph. Now, nine
years are gone, and the edge of that lake seems
nearer me. Your T-shirt shines, a white flake
on dark boulders; you wait beside the waves.

I try to frame it all, before it fades:
that place where cicadas sing forever.

Paris Notes

A trombonist stood, still and thin, playing
for the river; his jacket, improvised,
loose, floated on his shoulders. No paying
customers, just some bits of be-bop prised
from a blue sky. An organ moaned a low
celebration in Notre Dame's Gothic gloom
but in the sun someone began to blow
high spry notes from a bagpipe, making room
to jig as drums thrummed through the afternoon.
Later, I strolled in a Renoir then played
the lover lost in a ballad of moon
and April by Sinatra. A man laid
a rose on Piaf's grave; Jim Morrison's fans
crouched by a shrine of litter, bottles, cans.

Break

The wood-pigeons crashed like cannonballs;
the spiders' clinging strands stroked at our cheeks,
our lips. We eyed the pale slices of fungus.
Summer hung like glints in high windows
as we climbed up and through the old woods' twilight.

Beyond the trees' shade,
on a bare cliff-brink,
we stood miles above
a valley, glad of
the light
and an outlook.

But we knew we'd push back through the shadows
and, sinking into years of leaves, slither
down the crumbling slopes, the soft
moss-bandaged walls. And we knew we'd bolt
the shutters shut, tight against the night
then await the loudest sighs and creaks,
the black trees' softest cries; we knew
that, outside, the rubber toads would watch
their prey in silence as the big moths crowded
the lamp
and the dead leaves came under the door.

Oradour[*]

Oradour has no welcomes left; its stilled
streets are uneasy with visitors. Smiles
are out of place in Oradour. Sunlight
falls hard against its broken-teeth skyline.

In 1944 some soldiers came;
they herded, roasted, gunned in Oradour;
and, with wine upon their dribbling lips, sang
besotted praises to the mounting flames.

And no more bread was baked in Oradour.
Now people come to gaze at monuments;
they think of Germans and dead French children,
and if they should take a picture or two.

I wondered too. And was I a pilgrim,
or just a voyeur? Among the scorched walls,
inside the gates of Oradour, I felt
our ancient guilt, beneath a dark cold sun.

---

[*]On 10th June 1944 a German SS division massacred the population (including 247 schoolchildren) of Oradour-sur-Glane, near Limoges. The village has been conserved in its ruined state as a stark memorial.

At Wordsworth's Cottage

I have seen the skates you wore
to cut across the moon;
and in a lit glass case
your steel tooth-scrapers gleam.

You wrote of revolutions
in your neat brown-varnished room;
and you strode the fells at midnight,
fretted over postage costs.

You sang the tumbling tunes
of Helvellyn's mountain torrents
then lined your children's bedroom walls
with pages from The Times.

And now you are an industry:
your dear, dear sister
is a blank-eyed Dorothy doll.
The car people shuffle by.

And while you talked of joy,
the spirit and all nature's mysteries,
I think you might have warmed
to our swift turnstile efficiency.

Irina

They spoiled your liver, lungs, your kidneys, heart
and ovaries; they almost froze the life
from you because your work, the truth, your art
was deemed a crime against their State. Your life
was pierced with needles. And now your brain bursts
with a thousand remembered pains as you
live a kind of freedom, telling of thirsts,
of hungers and humiliations. You
who have worlds shining from your eyes had dreams
of a cherry-red dress as you pulled on
your anorak and canvas boots. It seems
to me you'll get your dress and slip it on
as, unafraid, you didn't give up hope
when picking out the truth on bits of soap.

I Fear

Some poets lose teeth and waste away; their veins
run slow with ice and chemicals. Beatings
are more routine than meals; yet all the pains,
all the blinding, torch-torn, midnight meetings
and probing wires that sear in secret places
won't make these poets say they aren't poets. Me?
I pen a line or two, go through my paces:
there's love, there's nature, war, perhaps a tree.
But would I face the locked steel door and fight
for truth behind barbed wire? I fear I might
stumble, compromise. I fear I wouldn't write.

The Catch

With a new fishing-net
and a boy's optimism
I probed the green pond to get
my very own wriggling minnows.

Now I dredge the shallows
of my thoughts for vital gleams
and glistening phantoms. It then goes
down on A4; and there it lies.

"Where do you get
your ideas?" folk say.
"I don't know," but today
I recalled a small silvery fish
floating, hard on the surface,
in an ornamental crystal dish.

Travelling

There are nomads and there are farmers. I
am much in love with journeying in life;
a poet, a true original with my
roots ripped up, my bed the edge of a knife,
I must be classless, atheistic. Love
must be fleeting and snatched from the wind, lost
then rhapsodised upon – a cold dove
in autumn leaves. I mustn't count mere cost:
my singularity is all as I run
alone to find the greenest sweet pastures.
But when I pass a lighted house, as sun-
light thins over ordered fields, the warmth lures
me; and security, pension, a car.
I panic at the thought of travelling far.

Going To Write

Each blank new day he enters the room; he
enters it alone. Some characters chat,
their hubbub bubbles as he hunts to see
a friendly face. He thinks of this and that
then smooths his lapels and straightens his tie.
He may drift, clearing his throat, towards two
lovers then, tongue-tied, pass silently by
to get himself a drink. "What do you do?"
a voice asks. He says nothing. And wonders
why he will accept these invitations
when mostly he just mutters and blunders
and grabs in despair for conversations.
At times he'd like to turn and run away,
not try to reach these strangers every day.

The Fly In The Poetry Book

The pages reflected the sunlight, flung
it into my narrowing eyes. Black words
melted, streamed around the gleam, as I clung
to the neat booklet, smelt blossom, heard birds.
A tiny fly, smaller than a rhyme, sprang
onto someone's so exact villanelle;
she scuttered diagonally, casual as slang,
flittering her feelers, scanning pell-mell.
Backwards and crossways, mingling her progress
with metaphors, she became all my day.
Her wings were finer than paper, had less
presence than moments, yet she shot away
in no time at all and became a part
of my pullover, somewhere near my heart.

Creative Writing

"And what is rhythm?" asks Janine, as Harry
(an experimentalist) rolls nose, blows
eyes. Prunella plans a life of Larry
Olivier, but has problems with her prose.
"Ye cannae beat Burns, if ye ask me," states
wee Tam, unasked. "I've *no* time for rhyme," drawls
languid Dolores. "Deep feeling negates
the need for form," she purrs deep in her shawls.
I smile, agree, and introduce the nuts
and bolts of verse, of plot, of dialogue;
and Hadrian's haiku needs a few cuts,
and I don't know a good rhyme for hedgehog.
But, later, slipping homewards in the train
a harp sings soft, unfingered, in my brain.

Evening Out

We talk of meals and compact discs;
we finish off another bottle.
But what of the raven with needle eyes?
His clattering wings are dark as death.

Yes, we did this and we saw that
and how your eyes glaze over.
Oh, you saw this and you did that?
And what of the raw baggage of our souls?

Then, goodbye all, we'll meet again
(as soon as we can take some more).
I'll tinker with the jangling bits,
type the madness into control.

He Once Was A German Lad

His cold wings of dark leather cast
deepening shadows on the camp.
No anaesthetic as the angel slit;
no antiseptic as the angel tied.
He laid his patients out,
shaven then incontinent:
his chosen ones.
Blood-smirched he probed
for perfection. The angel
fingered; the angel amputated.

Did that pale knifeman
hear the screams as he stooped
to his tasks with twilight
coldly flickering in his eyes?
And what strange gods devised him
then led him to a garden
to grow older?
It's said he once was a German lad
who ran through the cornfields of summer.
But that was centuries before
Mengele the bestial
angel of death
slouched towards Auschwitz
bearing gifts of pain.

Golgotha

We accepted the gifts
from the wise men in winter.

We ingested the flocks
from off the green hills;
the lamb slid easily
across our tongues.
We feasted with the darkest wine
as the babes grew strange.

We kissed beneath the elder trees
as the sunsets grew redder than poppies.

And when God's silver missiles
hiss across this planet of skulls,
we will have betrayed
ourselves, have nailed ourselves
bloodlessly to the world.
And there will be no crosses.

You Will Be Remembered

I, Herod Antipas, have sinned and sinned
again. I have lain with my dead brother's
wife, my jewel Herodias; when the torches
are extinguished and, at the darkest hour,
we lie in unlawful union, I swear
I feel his hand, cold upon my shoulder.

We sin; John the Baptist said thus but I
have silenced him forever and satisfied
divine Herodias. The prophet's hewn head,
streaming blood, was brought before us all, held
high upon a gleaming salver. Salome
looked away; she could not face those dead eyes
or gaze upon his clotted hair and beard.
Oh Salome, perfect daughter of my dark
pearl Herodias. Salome my niece,
step-daughter and dead brother's child, your dance
bewitched me; I could have given you half
a kingdom but your mother bade you ask
me for the head of John the Baptist. And
I had to give you what you asked of me;
you danced and danced so perfectly before
me. Your eyes outshone the golden borders
of your thin silk drapes. Your jewelled anklets paled
against the radiance of your faultless skin;
your young body swayed, it rose and fell; your
soft bare feet, the glimpses of your flesh –
what could I do? What *can* I do? I had
to yield to your desire, your stated wish.

Now Herodias is satisfied but I,
Herod Antipas, live on in sin. I,
though, will be forgotten while you Salome,
beloved niece, step-daughter and dead
brother's child, you will be remembered; you,
the dancing, sensual, beguiling girl.

The Dove

We saw a dove in a December tree;
he stared, he didn't move.

Isn't he pretty, we thought,
seeing his markings, his still dignity.

He stared, he didn't move;
then we saw the dried blood.

We saw the dried blood and the pellet-hole
in the dove in the December tree.

He stared into nothing, waiting,
ignoring the pellet-hole, the streaks of red.

We left him there and had our winter walk;
we saw the cold sky, the empty trees.

And we knew he would drop without ceremony
from his prime into the frost.

We stared at the red sun, the horizon.
It got colder and we kept moving.

Dried Flowers

In her room
she has some yellow dried flowers
in a cold glass decanter;
their heads are small as seeds,
quite juiceless; and they grow dusty.
Sometimes she rains hot breath on them,
makes them rustle like an old wedding-dress.

She has sat in there
all seasons staring
on dark days as rainwater
played, tumbling over her skylight.
And she has drunk blood-coloured wine
that left her parched,
sapped and counting anniversaries.

She has no children,
didn't want them. Her immortality
is lines like these
which crawl, crying occasionally,
over leaves of paper.
When the ink dries
it becomes quiet again
in there
except for the flowers rustling.

Leaving The Supermarket

She tucks her milk in, close beside the bread;
she's gentle with the eggs. Slowly, counting cost,
she fills her shopping-bag on wheels. She fed
a family long ago; they went, were lost
like the days and years when the corner shop
had everything and everyone was her friend.
She spreads a plastic bag across the top
to keep the contents safe and dry; each end
lies silky-smooth and neat. And all around
the cars speed off, packed with kids and hard brown
boxes. "Now here we go," she smiles. Playground
echoes dance in her brain; the dull grey town
is coloured again. "See the great big tram!"
she laughs, stepping proudly behind her pram.

Wintertime

The night ice oozes thickly through the blood.
Frost crumbles leaves; the reeds stand hard as spears
The hills are silent, fleeced with snow. An owl
is watching, still as stone, for prey; the old
man dreams, his skull all echoes with the sound
of closing doors; his bony feet lie white,
and cold as the roots of leafless trees. Night
is all; no gleam or moonbeam lights the ground.
Deep in his bed the old man grabs a hold
of the sheet. The night beasts snuffle; they prowl
the dark beyond his door. And then, no fears:
the night ice oozes thickly through the blood.

How Will I Know Spring?

It's mild today: the weather's nothing much.
A January sun, low, rolls red across
a southern sky. There's no iron hardness,
no frost like stone. I feel a soft strange loss.

And if I miss the snow's sifting silence
and east winds like honed blades, and if the cold
can't clutch and squeeze my bones, then how will I
know spring? Sweet frost must freeze and still the old

the withered, and dark clouds smother the land.
For then I can look for the trickling thaw,
a pulse, a reawakening. I can't live
without rebirth; I wait for winter's claw.

Sun And Candlelight

When sunlight thins
and warmth gives way
to slow, sharp icicles,
then shadow will spread
all down our walls,
as limbs grow colder.

Yet, when the ground
is iron, the sky steel,
we'll step into the air
of frozen night,
dazzled by the blaze
of dying candlelight.

Out In The Suburbs

Mild sunlight decorates
tree, bush and shrub. And all
is splendid silence. Gates

stand tight in hedge or wall;
doors are bright, handles shine
yet no-one comes to call.

White roses bloom in line;
their smell is mixed with scents
of polish and weak pine

disinfectant. Crescents
and Drives, Parks and Rises,
calm as convalescents'

homes. And no surprises
mar the outlook. TV
antennae, all sizes

and shapes, slice the sky. Tea-
time brings motors gliding
home; the thrush in the tree

keeps still, like stone. Sliding
garage doors click shut. Night
sneaks up as residing

goes on by shaded light,
behind soft curtains. Stars
glitter prettily, night

goes then morning-cold cars
cough slowly awake, hum
off to town. Nothing mars

the suburban morn. Some
birds poke the lawn and street;
again no callers come.

All is peace, almost sweet;
trim trees, the shrubs and birds
are in gardens as neat
as completed crosswords.

The Public Gardens Were Busy

The faintly clean smell of babies
rose from the tall black pram. Milky
gurglings spilled into the summer;
silky coverlets stirred, ruffled

by a listless breeze. Two small boys
played soldiers, until one cried. Cool
as an advert, the young man wore
his Walkman: tschi tschi tschi went his

afternoon. He absorbed the rich girl
through his sunglasses. Slowly, to
ensure the perfect tan, she moved
her heavy necklace. Then her arm

collapsed in the grass. Mum was lost
in Cosmopolitan. Should she
wear her hair streaked? Could she really
be bothered? With his empty pipe

clenched between his dentures, the old
man stared from his bench. His paper
lay unread; a fly examined
his eyebrow. The public gardens

were busy. A single leaf dropped
from an oak; a cloud passed over
the sun; some crows rose up screeching
towards the sky and, near the gate,
two gaunt dogs began to copulate.

In The Garden

She reads; a blackbird stabs
the earth beside her foot.
The sun glares white,
relentlessly; words run.
Warm breezes slip
through the undergrowth,
ruffling, softly fingering.
She turns a page,
shooing away an arching wasp.
Slow drops of perspiration
grow; he peels clingfilm
from his lunch-break apple,
murmuring lovely, lovely;
he watches her, then bites
and savours, brushing
against limp rhododendrons,
red as open wounds.

The Specialist

He stands with the men, shoulder to shoulder;
expressionless, they eye the magazines. Male
Interest is the thing they mostly crave: soft
pink dolls for their hard desires. The bolder

men reach out, fondle the pages. But he
has specialist interests, tastes; not for him
the swollen breasts, the satin straps. His hand
goes out to Health & Beauty: soon he'll see

glowing photos of perfect families
naked on the sand. But first, with quickening
step, he visits Mothercare; amongst tall
prams and furry bears he casually lays

his hand upon the glossy catalogue,
and is gone. In his still room he'll wonder
at the dimpled seductiveness of babes,
detect the yearning in their eyes. Again

he'll wonder why the world thinks it so bad
to feel just what he feels. It makes him sad
that he can't have a piece of harmless fun;
he'd love to love a pretty little one.

Gent

He follows me with eyes like fish.
The men, the boys come and go; he
stands, shuffles, stands amongst rubbish,

girls ripped from magazines, tissues.
How many anxious hours of life
has he glanced at backs, watched his shoes?

No pub, no restaurant: just a damp,
piss-smelling cave below the street.
Caged in wire, the yellowing lamp

is his candlelight as he waits
and waits for some reaction. Five
fast minutes with a stranger; dates

with boys in need of a buck. Such
is his love-life, his stealthy romance.
I rinse my hands briskly and clutch

at the towel; I don't once meet
his gaze; I climb up to the street,
the light. He stays, looking for love,

someone kind to come from above.
The water trickles as he waits
quietly holding back the floodgates.

The Night Gates

My skin is stroked by the ocean;
my hair is shimmering fronds,
serpentine and undulating.
Wonders flood into my eyes,
drench my senses as I whirl
through a star-flecked maelstrom,
writhe against the sand-grains'
brightest storm;
then the sea wafts me
easily
to where the corals lie.

(I breathe without equipment.)

The reef rises, almost enfolds me;
it is soaked in blood more red
than poppies; it is more daffodils
than yellow, more sky than blue.

I am dying to touch
the wavering coral garden
but currents squeeze my arms
to my sides. The sea screams
its song persistently.
I am dying
to clasp the dazzling
paint-box fossils,
that skeletal Eden.

But the dead light
breaks through my eyelids;
I am washed up
on the mattress.

The night gates have opened
and morning trickles slowly into me.

The Beasts

The colourless slugs come out at night;
they range beyond my closed doors,
graze, with all the time in the world,
on pieces of unpleasantness and moss.
I would not squeeze their moist softness
even for riches beyond my dreams.

The beasts slide through my nights, horns waving.
I wake each day and face their tangled trails.

Dream

I'd write you a house with ivied towers,
compose soft doves to brood in whispering
elms. I'd paint you all the summer flowers
to fill our endless garden. And I'd bring
golden leaves that wouldn't die, sweet sadness
without pain. We'd dance upon a lawn
in moonlight and celebrate the madness.
I'd sing you perfect lullabies at dawn.